Presented To:

_____

Presented By:

_____

Date:

_____

SEE IT-SAY IT
BIBLE STORYBOOK

Written by Anne Adams
Illustrated by Rick Incrocci

FaithKidz®

Equipping Kids for Life

COOK COMMUNICATIONS MINISTRIES
Colorado Springs, Colorado • Paris, Ontario
KINGSWAY COMMUNICATIONS LTD
Eastbourne, England

Faith Kidz® is an imprint of
Cook Communications Ministries, Colorado Springs, CO 80918
Cook Communications, Paris, Ontario
Kingsway Communications, Eastbourne, England

The See It, Say It Bible Storybook
© 2002 by Cook Communications Ministries

Previously published as *My Picture Bible Storybook*
First Faith Kidz edition titled *The See It, Say It Bible Storybook* published in 2006

First Printing, 2006
Printed in Korea
1 2 3 4 5 6 7 8 9 10 Printing/Year 11 10 09 08 07 06

ISBN: 0-781-4403-9 (hardcover)

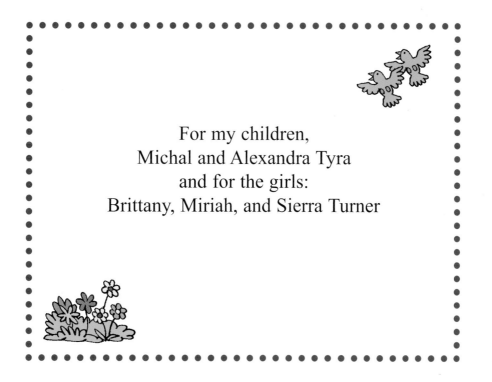

For my children,
Michal and Alexandra Tyra
and for the girls:
Brittany, Miriah, and Sierra Turner

Contents

birds · children · flowers · leaves · trees

God Made the World

Long ago, before the world was made, everything was dark and empty and very quiet. There were no 🐦 to sing. There were no 🧒 to play. There were no 🌸 to smell. 🍂 did not flutter in the breeze because there were no 🌳. There was nothing to hear, nothing to see, nothing to smell, nothing to taste, and nothing to feel. There was nothing at all.

God decided to fill up the empty. First, he made the huge. He made the ⊕ round like a ball and hung it inside the sky. The ≈≈ he formed were wide and deep. Next, he made the day and the night. He looked all around. It was good, but it was still too empty. Next he made trees and plants which grew yummy 🍓 and 🥕 .

stars planets fish birds bugs

God liked what He saw and kept going. He tossed and into the sky so the heavens would twinkle with lights. He reached deep into the sea and landed it with of dazzling colors and shapes. of all sizes spread their new wings with joy. They flew from the trees and even munched on some .

10

elephants

polar bears

monkeys

horses

tigers

Then came every kind of land animal. thundered across plains and crashed through forests. walked across ice in the coldest parts of the new earth. swung through the jungle on long vines. There were wild who galloped in herds and striped who hunted when the sun went to bed. God was pleased with his creation, but he knew that something was still missing.

11

streams   bees   tulips   man   woman

The First Man and Woman

Since the new earth was filled with creatures and plants of every kind, it was no longer so quiet and empty. Beautiful sounds and scents floated through the air. ⬡ bubbled up from beneath the ground. 🐝 hovered over bright 🌷 . *"Bzzz. Bzzz."* But it still wasn't quite right. God knew he needed a 👦 and a 👧 to take care of all of this creation. He got to work right away.

12

He scooped up some dust from the earth and shaped it into the form of a man. He named this first man Adam. He planted a lovely called Eden, so the man had his own place to live and work. Then he created the first woman, named Eve, so the man had a friend and helper. Adam and Eve were very happy. They drank from a sparkling and ate good food like , , and .

13

The First Sin

Each morning in the garden of Eden, the woke up

Adam and Eve with its warm rays. They had a lot of chores to

do to keep the garden looking beautiful, so they always started

early. Adam worked in the soft soil and trimmed the . Eve

gathered the ripe fruits and vegetables in she made out

of and .

14

| garden | Adam | Eve | finger | snake |

In the middle of the was a tree that carried a special ripe and juicy fruit. and walked around it, careful never to lay a on it. They remembered God's words: "You can eat from any tree except this one. If you do, you will surely die." Then one day, the Devil, dressed up like a sneaky , slithered through the garden in search of . On that day, everything changed forever.

15

"Hi ," said the snake, pretending to be her friend.

"Doesn't this look yummy? If you eat it, you won't die.

You'll get really super smart like God." thought about that.

The did look really good. And it would be nice to be super

smart. Maybe if she just took a *little* bite, God wouldn't mind.

She picked a piece and held it up to her . Her

sank into the sweet and juice dripped down her .

16

It tasted so good; she gave a bite. At that instant, they knew they had disobeyed God and sinned for the first time. They were very ashamed. God made them 👚👗 and sadly sent them out of the garden. As 👁 streamed down their 😟, Adam and Eve said good-bye to all of the 🐘🦒 that were their friends. They left to find their new home.

17

| baby | sheep | goats | cabbage | peas |

Two Brothers

Adam and Eve were finally settled in their new home beyond the garden of Eden. It wasn't long before Eve gave birth to a boy named Cain and to another boy named Abel. When they were grown, Abel worked in the field taking care of flocks of and . Cain was a farmer. He worked in the soil growing crops like and .

One morning, the two brothers decided to give a to

God. Abel was excited. He loved God so much; he wanted to

please him with the best gift of all. He went to his flock and

picked out the biggest and fattest . God will like this! he

thought. Cain wanted to please God, too, but he was in a hurry.

He quickly ran into the and scooped up some

from the dirt and picked some .

19

When the brothers gave their to God, they learned that Abel's 🐑 pleased God the most. Cain was mad. He squinted his 👀 and rolled his hands into tight 👊👊. "I know I didn't give God the best present," he muttered, "but I won't say I'm sorry. I just won't." Instead, he put his hand on his brother's 🫳 and said, "Abel, how about we take a little walk?"

20

They walked far into the field, away from the family and the where they got their water. was mad at his brother. He turned to his brother and killed him. On that sad day, God sent away from his home. He wandered about for a long time. Later, he built a new to to because he could never go back to his home again.

The Big Flood

Years after God made Adam and Eve, the was filled

with lots of . It wasn't a nice place anymore.

and stole things, told lies, cheated, and even hurt one

another. They didn't want to pray to God and please him. In the

entire world, there was only one man left who still loved God.

His name was .

22

God knew the only way to save the world was to wipe out everything in it and start all over again. Since Noah still loved God, he decided to spare him and his . "Build a really, really, big ," God whispered in his . "Go inside of it with your , two of every creature, and lots of and ."

23

When the ark was built, Noah stood at the door while his family went inside. Storm were gathering above, and everyone was in a hurry. flew in quickly. used their necks to try to push ahead. The snapped at the slow-moving turtles. A pair of carpenter carried bits of bread in case they got hungry. Creatures walked, crawled, flew, hopped, and even squirmed into the ark.

24

Noah   raindrops   puddles   lakes   mountains

Just as followed them in, God shut the door, and the clouds burst open. Big fell from the sky for forty days and forty nights. turned into rivers, which turned into until even the were covered by a gigantic ocean. The only thing left was t... which floated peacefully on the smooth water.

After many months, God sent a strong to sweep away the water like a big broom. Noah saw the again for the first time since ... f the flood. He opened the

 of the ark and fil ... gs with fresh air. Then, he

sent out a ... to see if the water

had dr ...

26

The dove flew back to the window of the ark with a

tender olive in its . Noah knew the ground must

be dry if and were sprouting again. He opened

the for the first time si   starte . He and his

family and all of the creat   little, stepped out. It
was time to start over   utiful e rth.

flood   houses   roads   muscles   backs

The Tall Tower

Now that the big was gone, Noah and his family made a fresh start on the new earth. Noah's children had lots of children. Their children had lots of children. More and more people spread out across the land. They worked hard and built houses to live in and roads to travel on. Their muscles bulged, and their backs ached.

28

They looked at their new city. "It's not special enough," they said. "We need to build something amazing so we will be famous. Then no one will forget us." So they made a bunch of 🧱 and began to build a tall 🏗 . They put gooey 🔴 between the bricks to make them stick together. They climbed on 🪜 and tried to stretch the tower all the way to the ⭐ .

29

The beat on their backs during the day, but they would not stop working. At night, they built under the light of the . Their were sore, and their hands were rough with . They looked at their new city again, and this time they were amazed. "Wow!" they said. "Look at this super cool we've built with our own hands. Maybe we don't really need God after all."

30

The voices of the men were carried into and reached the 🪑 of God. He came down to visit the 🏙️ and he saw the tower the men built. God knew it was dangerous for the people to think they did not need him. He touched every man's 👅 so they spoke different languages. He scattered them over the 🌍. They learned that they needed God because they couldn't rely upon each other anymore.

31

night   lamps   path   gate   angels

Two Bad Cities

At the twin cities of Sodom and Gomorrah glowed with the light of shining . Two men walked quietly on a toward the city . Lot watched the men approach. He loved God, and he knew right away that these men were really . He bowed low with his face to the ground. "Please," he said, "spend the night at my house." The angels agreed.

He baked and made his heavenly guests a delicious . Later, as the angels got ready for , evil men from both cities came to the . Lot went outside quickly and shut the door behind him. "Where are the men who are staying with you?" they yelled. "Bring them out so we can hurt them." They beat on the and tried to break it down.

33

| angels | eyes | family | dawn | hands |

Suddenly, the appeared in the doorway. They pulled Lot inside and blinded the men's so they couldn't find the door. "Listen," they whispered to Lot, "this city is filled with such evil, the Lord has sent us here to destroy it. Take your and leave at once." When arrived and Lot had not left yet, the angels took his and those of his wife and daughters and led them safely out of the city.

34

legs   statue   salt   ashes   smoke

"Now, run for your lives," the angels cried. "Don't stop or you will be swept away. Whatever you do, *don't look back.*" Lot and his family ran as fast as their could carry them. But as his wife turned to peek over her shoulder, she was instantly changed into a of because she looked back at the city. The next morning, two piles of and plumes of were all that remained of the two bad cities.

35

coat   sleeves   rainbow   thread   ribbon

The Coat of Many Colors

Jacob was an old man when his wife Rachel gave birth to
Joseph, his eleventh son. He loved all of his sons very much, but
Jacob gave Joseph more love and attention than any of the
others. One day he made his son a beautiful . It had long
flowing , colors like a , and was sewn with silky
and .

36

Joseph's brothers knew their father loved Joseph the best.
Some of them were very jealous. They were in the
tending the when they spotted Joseph walking past a pile
of . "There he is," they said to each other. "There's our
father's favorite son. Let's kill him and throw him into a .
We'll say that a wild tore him to pieces."

37

well   arms   shoulders   coat   water

Reuben, Joseph's oldest brother, heard this talk. "Look," he reasoned, "there's no need to kill him. Let's just throw him into the ." He secretly hoped to rescue his little brother and take him home to Jacob. When Joseph came near, they grabbed him roughly by the and . They tore off his beautiful and threw him into the well, which was empty of .

lunch   camels   money   coat   Joseph

The brothers sat down to eat their as a caravan of passed by. "Hey," said another brother, "I have the best idea of all. Let's sell to this caravan and get some for him." While Reuben was away, they dragged Joseph to the caravan owners and traded him. They splashed his with animal blood, brought it to their father, and told him that was dead. Jacob cried for a very long time.

39

feet   desert   sandals   sun   sand

Joseph and the King

The instant Joseph was sold to the merchant caravan, he became a slave. For days, he dragged his sore behind the camels as they traveled through the dusty to Egypt. His were falling apart, and he no longer had his coat to protect him from the and flying . He felt alone and afraid and very, very sad.

king   ring   finger   chain   hand

God was with Joseph in Egypt! He worked so hard through the years that the made him the ruler of the whole country! He gave Joseph a special to wear on his , beautiful linen robes, and a gold to hang around his neck. He told Joseph, "I may be the king, but without your word, no one in Egypt may lift a or a foot."

Together Again!

For seven years the fields of Egypt grew more food than the people could eat. There were and of grain all over the place. Joseph took the extra food and stored it in the cities so it would not go to waste. Then fields everywhere stopped growing food. of grain died in the scorching sun. would not sprout. Not a single could be grown anywhere.

42

food　　donkeys　　ten　　money　　grain

In every country except Egypt, the people were so hungry their stomachs hurt. When news spread that Egypt had stored , men climbed on their 🫏 and headed to Egypt. Jacob, Joseph's father, gave his 🔟 sons some 🪙. "Go down to Egypt and buy some ⛰ for us," he told them. "If you do, maybe we won't die after all."

43

ring   chain   tears   heart   money

Joseph was at the food counter when his brothers arrived. He was wearing his royal robes, , and . They did not know who he was, but Joseph knew them. His eyes filled with , and his rejoiced even though they had hurt him long ago. He filled their sacks with grain and put their back inside their bags.

44

When was sure his brothers had changed their ways, he told them who he was. "Go home right away and tell my father I am still alive," he said. "Then bring him here to me." For the first time in many years, Joseph wrapped his around his father's soft . A lit up his . "God has brought us back together," he told Jacob and his brothers. "I hope we will never be apart again."

45

| king | throne | scroll | baby | river |

Baby Moses

Lots of Israelites moved to Egypt during the big famine when there was no food. After Joseph died, a very mean came to power. He hated God, and he hated all of God's people that lived in his country. He sat on his one day and pulled out a . "All Israelites shall become slaves of Egypt," he announced meanly. "And all boys shall be tossed into the Nile ."

46

3				
three	basket	blanket	reeds	hands

Soon after, Moses was born. His mother loved him very much, and she could *never* throw him into a river. She hid him for **3** months. When he was too big to hide, she put him in a and covered him with a . Gently, she lowered the basket into the at the river's edge and watched it float downstream. She clasped her together. "Lord," she prayed, "please take care of baby Moses."

47

Miriam, Moses' sister, crept among the tall and watched her baby brother from a safe distance. She saw bounce softly in his . He floated right to the , where the king's daughter, the , was bathing in the water. When the princess heard the baby cry, she plucked the basket out of the river at once.

The princess loved Moses right away. She knew by the of his that he was an Israelite baby. "Poor little one," she said as she rubbed his . "If I don't do something, you will die." The princess agreed to let Moses' mother care for him when he was small. When Moses was a young man, he moved to the and lived like an Egyptian for a time.

palace   sheep   desert   mountain   fire

The Burning Bush

Moses was all grown up when he left his life forever. He returned to his own people, the Israelites, and became a simple shepherd. One day, he led his to the far edge of the near the big of God. He was resting in the shadows when he saw a bright out of the corner of his eye.

50

Moses moved closer to have a better look. He noticed that hot orange **flames** were shooting out of a **bush**, but the **branches** were not burning! Then he heard God's voice call to him from within the fire. He caught his breath. "Yes! Here I am, Lord!" he answered in a tiny voice. He took off his **sandals** and bowed low with his **face** to the ground.

tears   milk   honey   ears   mouth

"I see the of my people in Egypt," God said. "Tell the king to let my people go. Take them to a land flowing with milk and honey." Moses could not believe his ears. How could *he* lead thousands of Israelites out of Egypt? "Lord," Moses said, "you know I'm not a great speaker." God replied, "I know, I know. Take your brother, Aaron, with you. He speaks well. He will be your mouth."

52

king staff snake Moses mountain

"Lord," said, "what if the does not believe it was *you* who sent me?" God replied, "Take out your / and throw it to the ground." Moses did, and his staff turned into a slithering . God said, "I will perform miracles such as these, . You won't be alone. Go at once. Return with my people to worship me on this ." Moses left to do what God had asked.

53

palace   door   desert   king   heart

Ten Terrible Plagues

Moses and Aaron went to the royal in Egypt and
knocked on the . "Listen up!" Aaron told the king. "God
says, 'Let my people go so they may worship me in the .'"
"Listen up!" the told Aaron. "I say NO!" The Lord saw
that the king's was turned against him, so he stretched
out his hand over Egypt. Ten terrible plagues fell upon the
country, one after another.

fish   frogs   beds   bowls   ovens

First came the plague of blood. All of the water in the Nile River turned to beet-red blood. The died, the water smelled very stinky, and the people had nothing to drink. Next, thousands of frogs hopped out of the river. They jumped into the people's homes and into their beds when they were asleep. They bounced into mixing bowls and even into the ovens.

Then swarms of and swirled over the land and covered it like a blanket of dust. The , , , goats, and sheep died. God did not allow any of these plagues to harm his people, but there wasn't a single Egyptian who did not suffer. Still, the king was stubborn and would not let the Israelites go. "I still say NO!" he said. The plagues continued.

ashes   snow   sky   lightning   hail

Moses scooped from a furnace and tossed them into the air. A fine powder floated down, like ❄ , and horrible sores broke out on all of the Egyptians. Then the ☁ split open. Thunder shook the earth, ⚡ lit the dark, and huge balls of 🌨 fell from the clouds. Anyone who was outside during the terrible hailstorm was killed. Still, the king said NO! so the plagues continued.

| wind | locusts | grass | moss | leaf |

A mighty east blew across Egypt all day and all night. By morning, hungry covered the ground until it was black. Every blade of , every piece of , every was gobbled up. When the locusts flew away, an eerie darkness covered Egypt. For three days, the sun did not shine. In all of the country, only the Israelites had light.

lamb	door	shadow	house	king

The tenth and last plague was the worst one of all. God told the Israelites to smear the blood of a on the tops and sides of every ⬜ . At midnight, the Lord passed like a ➤ through each 🏠 *not* marked with blood. When the Lord left, every firstborn child or animal was dead. Only the Israelites were spared. Finally, the 👑 said to Moses, "I've had enough. Go! Take your people and leave me alone!"

59

Crossing the Sea

Moses and Aaron raced from the king's palace in darkness. "Quick!" they cried to the Israelites. "Get your children and your animals. We must leave *now*." The people hurried and grabbed whatever they could carry. The women balanced bread in upon their . They took their and some extra . Then thousands left to follow Moses into the wilderness.

They stayed together as they trudged through the 🌵. By day, God moved in front of them in the form of a white ☁️. At night, he lit their way in a flaming column of 🔥. When they couldn't push their 👣 forward another inch, they made camp. The Red 〰️ was stretched out wide before them and the wilderness was behind them.

horse · hooves · chariots · soldiers · Moses

They had no sooner sat down to rest than a rumble of was heard. When they looked up, hundreds of and loomed on the horizon. They ran to . "We are doomed!" they cried. "The sea is in front of us and the Egyptians are behind. We can't escape!" quieted them with his words. "Don't be afraid! Stand firm and see how God will deliver you on this day!"

Moses lifted his over the , and a ferocious blew back the water and divided it in half. A of dry land appeared in the middle of the sea. "Come on! Let's go!" they called to one another. "God has made a way for us." They were surrounded on both sides by walls of water, and in the water they could see the swimming.

horses	chariots	horsemen	wheels	wind

The Israelites were ahead when God allowed the Egyptians to chase them into the sea. and and raced along the path. Then their flew off, and the chariots were stuck in the soft seabed. As the whistled again, the walls of water collapsed and sank back into the sea. Every soldier was trapped below, but all of God's people had made it safely to the shore.

| bread | quail | water | trees | mountain |

God's Law

The Israelites walked day and night through the wilderness, and God always cared for them. When they were hungry, rained from heaven and blew in with the wind. When they were hot and thirsty, he led them to springs of and shady . A month after leaving Egypt, they saw the peak of God's rising through the clouds. Moses brought them near the mountain, and they set up camp.

65

One morning, the mountain was covered with a thick

[cloud] . Smoke swirled from the peak to the [sky] . The people

trembled with fear when [lightning] flashed and the ground

beneath their feet shook with thunder. Inside the mist, an

angel blew a [trumpet] to announce the arrival of God. At that

instant, the Lord descended upon the mountain. [Moses] climbed

the steep slopes to meet with God.

The Israelites waited and waited for Moses to return. Finally, they got tired of waiting.

"Where is he?" they asked Aaron. "We don't think he's ever coming back." They took off their gold and tossed them into a big . Aaron took the gold, melted it down over a , and made a huge golden . Then they had a party. They ate lots of , did lots of dancing, and began to worship the instead of God.

67

As Moses made his way down the , he heard the
joyful shouts of the people. In his hands he held two stone
tablets upon which God had written his laws. When he neared
the camp, he saw the golden calf. His face was red with
rage. "How did this happen?" he asked Aaron. "I trusted you to
take care of things while I was away." Moses threw the tablets
to the ground, breaking them into lots of tiny pieces.

68

He grabbed the 🐐 and scorched it in the fire. Then he ground it into powder, scattered it on the water, and made the people drink it. Moses took a ⛏ and carved out two more stone 📖. He climbed the ⛰ again and spent forty days and forty nights without any food or water. After this time, God allowed Moses to write his laws on the new 📖. They were called the 🔟 Commandments.

saddle   donkey   road   tracks   tail

The Talking Donkey

Early one morning Balaam threw a over his and climbed onto her back. Together they traveled down a dusty dirt . Suddenly, the stopped in her and swished her . Just ahead, an angel stood in the road holding a long, silver sword. The quickly turned toward a field. Balaam never saw the angel. He mumbled under his breath and beat his hard for straying off the .

They continued their journey on a narrow , which ran between two lush . There were on both sides. Once again, the donkey looked up and saw the standing in the path. Since there was nowhere to run, she pressed tightly against the wall, smashing her master's . Balaam never saw the . "All right," he cried. "I've had enough of this nonsense." He beat her harder than before.

71

donkey   path   angel   sword   staff

The moved forward and the grew more narrow. One more time, she looked up to find the holding the shiny silver . There was no room to turn around and no room to the right or to the left. She had no choice but to lie down in the middle of the path. Still, Balaam did not see the angel. He was so angry he took out his and beat her harder than ever.

When the donkey felt the sting of the upon her

, she cried out in pain. "Why do you beat me like this,

master?" she asked through her . Balaam was surprised to

hear his donkey's voice. "You've made a fool of me!" he replied.

"If I had a sword in my hand, I'd kill you right now." The Lord

opened Balaam's . When he saw the angel for the first

time, he fell with his to the ground.

73

angel | path | donkey | three | sword

The stood still on the ▨ and looked at Balaam.
"Why have you beaten this poor animal?" he asked. "I've come to
deliver a message from God, and if your 🐴 had not turned
away from me these **3** times, I would have drawn my
🗡 and killed *you*." Balaam felt very, very bad and
realized he had sinned.

74

A City Falls Down!

The Israelites wandered in the for forty years. In the last year, Moses died and Joshua became the new leader. He led them to the land that God said flowed with and . For the first time in many years, they ate and that grew in the fields. They were very happy to be out of the wilderness.

They crossed the Jordan River and came to the city of Jericho. It was protected by huge over feet high. were perched on top of the . When they spotted the Israelites, they cried out, "Enemies below!" and were slammed shut and bolted. Jericho was locked up tight. No one went out and no one dared come in.

76

Then the Lord spoke to Joshua. "This 🏙, its 👑, and all of its fighting 👥 shall be yours. Do exactly as I say." Joshua gathered the Israelites around him and whispered God's plan. They nodded their 🧑. The next day, they lined up at the city 🚪 and waited. When Joshua saw that everyone was in place, he shouted, "Advance!" The soldiers and priests moved forward.

77

They marched around the city once as the [priests] blew

their [trumpets] . Then they returned to [camp] and spent the

night. Every day for six days, they circled the city just once. On

the seventh day, they rose with the [sun] , met at the [gate] ,

and waited. Joshua moved down the line and asked every man,

"Do you know the plan?" When he was sure they were ready,

he took a deep breath and cried, "Advance!"

Soldiers and priests moved forward and marched around the city 6 times. On the seventh time around, Joshua's voice rang out clear. "Shout, men! The Lord has given you the city!" They raised their voices loud, and the priests blew their hard. Suddenly, the walls began to crumble. fell to the ground in a of . The Israelites charged into Jericho shouting victory and captured it for the Lord.

David and the Giant

David was a young . He was in the fields tending when his father came to him. "David, since your brothers went to war, I've been worried sick. Take them some and a of grain. See how they're doing." Early in the morning, David left. When he arrived at the camp, he heard a deep voice rumble through the valley. "Hey, you little ! Bawk! Bawk! Can you hear me?"

80

On the other side of the was a named
Goliath who was more than nine feet tall! He was wearing a
bronze and a . He was waving a huge .
While David watched, Goliath cupped a hand to his mouth. "Didn't
anyone hear me? Which one of you scrawny chickens is going
to fight me?" Goliath laughed so hard his body shook and his
armor rattled. "You're not SCARED, are you?"

81

When the soldiers heard Goliath's words, they began to shake in their . David looked at them. "You are God's people. How can you allow this rotten giant to talk to you that way?" he asked. "If no one here will fight him, then I will!" David took his and his . He chose five smooth from the and put them in his shepherd's bag.

Then David crossed the 🌳 between the two 🏔 to meet the 🛡. Goliath took one look at him and sneered. "Does this boy intend to fight me with 🪵?" he bellowed. "Come here, kid, so I can feed you to the 🐦." David stood tall and proud. "Goliath," he answered, "you come against me with sword and spear, but I come against you in the name of the Lord."

| hand | bag | stone | forehead | giant |

As Goliath moved closer, David ran quickly toward the battle line to cut him off. He reached his small into his and pulled out a . Then he slung it with all his might at the giant. The stone sailed through the air and sank into Goliath's . He collapsed to the ground. The small shepherd had defeated the !

king	queen	statues	rain	clouds

Elijah and the Ravens

Elijah was a great prophet, and he loved God very much.

During his time a very wicked and ruled the land.

King Ahab and Queen Jezebel hated God. They worshipped

 and tried to make all of God's people worship them too.

God was angry with their sin. He held the in the

 for several years. The rivers and streams dried up, and

the food in the fields withered away.

85

God knew that 🧔 was good, and he wanted to take care

of him. "Leave this place," he told Elijah. "Go east and you will

find a small 🏞 near the Jordan River. Hide there. There

is a bubbling 🪨 that will wet your 👄 and quench

your thirst. Also, I have spoken to the 🐦 of the air. They

will feed you."

86

Elijah traveled to the valley. All around were dry, cracked riverbeds, but the stream God told him about still bubbled. He dipped his into the cool water and drank. In the mornings and evenings, black carried bits of and chunks of juicy in their . Elijah filled his empty stomach. He thanked God for caring for him, just as God always did!

| dock | boat | seas | wind | waves |

Jonah and the Big Fish

God knew the city of Nineveh was full of wicked people. "Go there," he told Jonah. "Tell the people to change their ways." Instead, Jonah ran away from God. He went to the 🏗 and got on a huge ⛵. It was sailing the 〰️ away from Nineveh. While he was on board, God sent a mighty 🌬️ to blow across the water. The 🌊 beat the hull and rocked the ship back and forth.

Black opened up and dumped onto the deck until it covered the sailors' . "All hands on deck!" shouted the captain. "We've got to lighten the load. Throw the cargo over before we drown!" Crates of and of food flew over the side. "Who is to blame for bringing this storm upon us?" the sailors cried above the noise of the wind. The captain went below deck to find Jonah.

The gathered around him. "Who are you?" they

asked. looked into their 👁👁. "I am an Israelite," he

replied. "I worship the Lord, the God of heaven who made the

sea and the land." The men were afraid then. "What have you

done to bring the 🌧 and 💨 upon us?" they asked.

 admitted that he had run away from God. "Toss me into

the sea, and your troubles will be over," he said.

The sailors lined up on either side of Jonah. They picked
him up and carried him across the on their .
"Heave ho!" they yelled and tossed him over. The instant Jonah
hit the water, the rain stopped, the waves sank into the sea,
and the wind slowed to a whisper. Jonah sank deeper and
deeper into the murky water. seaweed swirled around his head,
and schools of fish darted past his eyes.

91

fish   mouth   Jonah   sea   shore

When he thought he couldn't hold his breath for another moment, a huge 🐟 opened his 👄 and swallowed him whole. 🧔 floated into the fish's belly. It was cold and stinky, but it was safe. "Thank you, Lord, for saving me," he said over and over. Three days later, the fish rose to the surface of the 〰️ and spit Jonah out. He landed on a sandy 🏖️. Jonah decided that the next time God spoke, he would listen!

Three Men in a Furnace

King Nebuchadnezzar of Babylon had his on the city of Jerusalem. There were rumors that God's 🏛 was filled with golden 👼 , silver 🍷 , and rooms overflowing with 🪙 . He sent his soldiers to take the city. They raided the temple, stole the treasures, and captured the finest men. Three of those men were Shadrach, Meshach, and Abednego. They were hauled off to the king's palace.

93

The ordered a huge golden statue to be made. It was over ninety feet high and feet wide. He gathered the people. "When you hear the blast of a , the trill of a , or the ping of a ," he proclaimed, "you must bow down and worship my statue. If you don't, you will be thrown into a fiery furnace!"

harp   horn   flute   knees   throne

The very next day, the music of the , , and

 floated through the air. People everywhere stopped what

they were doing. They dropped to their and prayed to the

golden god. Shadrach, Meshach, and Abednego refused. They

were dragged to the king's . "It has been brought to my

attention that you refuse to bow down and worship my god,"

the king roared. "Is this true?"

95

The three men replied, "We will not serve your gods no matter what you do to us." The shook his . "Heat up the furnace **7** times hotter," he raged. Shadrach, Meshach, and Abednego were bound tight with and tossed into the . Later, the king peeked into the furnace. "What's this?" he cried. "I see four men instead of three. They are walking around unharmed, and one looks like the Son of God!"

96

He called to them, "Shadrach! Meshach! Abednego! Come out!" When the three men walked out of the , the king saw that their was not singed and their were not burned. "Praise the God of Shadrach, Meshach, and Abednego!" he cried. "He sent his to rescue these men." The king realized that no other god, not even his golden , could do what God did on that day.

97

temple   city   palace   king   magicians

The Writing on the Wall

Daniel was living in Jerusalem when the holy ▯ was raided and the ▯ conquered. He was captured and taken to the king's ▯ in Babylon, just like his friends Shadrach, Meshach, and Abednego. God made Daniel smarter and wiser than all of the king's men. Daniel told the ▯ the meaning of his dreams and visions when the king's own ▯ could not.

| tables | tablecloths | cups | temple | trays |

One evening the king had a huge feast. Thousands of people were seated at long with fine ___ . "Bring in the gold and silver ___ ," the king cried, "the ones my father stole from God's ___ ." The servants carried shiny ___ . On them were ___ filled with ruby-red wine. They passed around the ___ and drank. "Praise the gods of gold and silver!" they shouted merrily.

99

Suddenly, the of a human hand appeared and begin to write on the wall. The people grew quiet and stared. The king began to shake. His knocked together, and his felt weak. "Where are my ?" he asked frantically. When they arrived, he said, "Tell me what this message says, and you shall wear purple robes and gold ." Not one of the could read the writing.

100

| queen | robes | chain | neck | king |

The heard the noise and went to her husband. "Daniel, the Israelite, has the spirit of the holy gods in him," she said. "He can read this message for you." Daniel was brought to the king, and God allowed him to read the writing. He was clothed in purple . A gold was hung around his . "Hail to Daniel," the said. "He is now the third highest ruler in my kingdom!"

101

Daniel in the Lions' Den

The king thought was so wise, he planned to make him ruler of the whole . The other leaders were jealous. "That is not right!" said one. "He's an Israelite, and now he is going to be more powerful than us." They formed a and came up with a plan. "We'll convince the to make a new law," said another. "Whoever prays to any god or man, except the king, shall be tossed to the ."

They all cheered. "Good thinking!" they said. So the leaders went to the and told him about the idea. King Darius tapped his and thought about it for half a second. "Yes! I love the idea," he exclaimed. "Everyone can worship ME! Good thinking, men!" That day the royal scribe got out his and and put the law down on .

stairs room window three knees

Daniel heard about the new law. He went home and climbed the to his upper . Here, the faced the city of Jerusalem. **3** times a day, he bent to his and prayed to God, just as always. When the leaders found out Daniel was still praying, they got excited. "See!" they said. "He's breaking the law. Let's go tell the king."

King Darius was sitting on his when the men came in. "Oh king," they said, "your servant Daniel is not as wise as you thought. He was found breaking your new law." The king nodded his sadly. "Take him to the den of ," he muttered. Daniel was captured and thrown into the lions' . A big was rolled over the entrance so he couldn't escape.

105

At , the king awoke. "Please, oh please, oh please, let him still be alive," he mumbled as he hurried to the den. "Daniel!" he called. "Has your God rescued you?" He put his 👂 near the 🪨 "King!" Daniel called back. "My God sent an 👼 to shut the 👄 of the lions!" King Darius rejoiced as he pulled Daniel out. Soon after, he made a new law. Everyone must worship the God of Daniel—or else!

baby	donkey	room	inn	stable

Jesus Is Born!

"Hurry, Joseph!" Mary said as she rubbed her round belly. "I'm going to have this soon." Mary rode on a , and Joseph walked in front as they traveled to Bethlehem. Once they arrived, they couldn't find a place to stay. Every at every was full. Finally, Joseph found space in a . "I'm sorry, Mary," he said. "It's not a fancy place, but at least it's safe and warm."

baby   clothes   manger   hay   stars

A short time later, Mary gave birth to the Jesus. She wrapped him tenderly in swaddling and placed him in a . The sweet scent of hung in the air. Outside, glittered in the night sky. Mary watched her sleeping . She still couldn't believe that *she* was chosen to be the mother of the Son of God. "Truly, nothing is impossible with you, Lord," she murmured.

shepherds   sheep   angel   light   staffs

Nearby, were living in the fields. They were keeping watch over their at night. All at once, an appeared, and the of the Lord shone around the men. They were terrified, and some of them dropped their . "Don't be afraid!" the said. "I bring you joyful news! Today, in the town of Bethlehem, a Savior was born to you and all people. He is Christ the Lord!"

109

angels   wings   earth   hair   gold

A choir of flew from heaven and joined the one in the field. Their sparkled with silver dust, and their shone with strands of . They lifted their voices together and sang, "Glory to God in the highest, and on peace to all men!" The angels glided back to heaven, leaving the shepherds in the quiet night.

shepherds   baby   manger   Mary   Joseph

The stared at one another in amazement. "Let's go and see this Christ child," one said. They all agreed, and they hurried off to Bethlehem. When they found the lying in his and saw and beside him, they praised God. They traveled throughout the area and shouted the good news. "Our Savior is born! Our Savior is born! It is a day to rejoice!"

wise men	camels	deserts	mountains	star

Three Wise Men

Three rode into Jerusalem on their . They had traveled a long way through and over , and their journey wasn't over yet. "Please, where is the one who was born King of the Jews?" they asked around the town. "We saw his in the east, and we want to worship him."

King Herod heard that the were asking for Jesus, and he was furious. "Why are they calling *him* 'King of the Jews'?" he shouted, shaking his royal . "What am I? Chopped liver?" His servants bowed. "Oh no, sire," they replied. "You are the only real of the Jews." Herod had an idea. He sent for his . "Find the wise men," he ordered. "Invite them to the . I'd like a word with them."

113

| wise men | carpet | throne | King | three |

The arrived. They walked the red to the and bowed low. "You wished to see us, your royal highness?" one asked. Herod smiled wickedly. "I am desperate to worship this child everyone is talking about," he lied. "Find out where he is, report back to me, and I will be most grateful." The 3 men nodded and went on their way.

star   sky   gold   perfume   spices

As the wise men moved forward, a bright shone above. It lit the at night and led them to Bethlehem. It stopped just above the simple house where Jesus lived. When they saw him, they fell to their knees. "Praise to the little King," they cried with joy. They offered gifts of , , and . That night, they were warned in a dream not to see Herod. They took a different road home.

115

Escape to Egypt

The wise men climbed on their camels. They went home without stopping at the palace. When King Herod realized the men had tricked him, he was furious. He stomped his foot and called in his trusted advisors. "Does anyone know where this little King of the Jews is?" he demanded. The men shook their heads. "Well then," Herod reasoned, "if we can't find one boy, we'll have to kill *all* the boys."

116

angel   dream   Jesus   King   Mary

That night, an of the Lord came to Joseph in a . "Get up!" the said. "Go to Egypt with Jesus and his mother. Stay there until I tell you. Herod is looking for the child and wants to kill him." Joseph heeded the angel's warning. He got up right away and helped Jesus and get ready. They fled while it was still dark.

bed	dream	angel	Mary	king

The family stayed in Egypt for a long time. One night, while Joseph slept in his , the angel came to him in a dream again. The angel said, "Get up! Take Jesus and his mother and go back to Israel. It's safe now. King Herod is dead." Joseph nudged Jesus and Mary until they woke up. They gathered their things and left Egypt to return to their homeland.

118

John the Baptist

John the Baptist stood on a in the desert and stretched out his arms to the crowd gathered around him. "Repent! The kingdom of heaven is near," he cried. "Prepare the way for the Lord! Make a straight ⬚ for him!" Many shoved their way to the front to get a closer look at John. His clothes were made of coarse 🐪 hair, and they hung loosely from his shoulders. A worn leather ⬚ was tied around his ⬚.

119

hand   river   heart   head   smile

"Teacher!" an old man called. "Tell me what to do. I've been a sinner my whole life." John took the man by the and gently led him to the Jordan . "God hears your voice and sees your ," he said, placing his hands on the man's . John baptized him, and the old man climbed up the sandy shore. A huge stretched his wrinkled face.

John looked at the waiting on the as the water swirled around his 🦵. "Listen up, people!" he called. "One is coming who is more powerful than I am. I am not fit to carry even his 👡. I baptize you with water, but he will baptize you with the Holy Spirit and with 🔥."

saw in the Jordan and saw the rushing to get into the water. He waded in and stood before him. "John," he said, "it is I— . I've come to be baptized by you." lowered his and dropped his voice to a whisper. "Lord, I need to be baptized by *you*, and you are coming to me instead? I am not good enough to baptize my Lord."

put his hands on John's . "John," he said, "it is all right. It is God's will for you to do this thing." John nodded his and gently lowered into the cool water. As he came up, the heavens split open, and the Spirit of God came upon Jesus in the form of a . A voice from heaven said, "This is my Son, whom I love; with him I am well pleased."

123

The Devil Tempts Jesus

 walked far into the wilderness. For forty days and forty nights, he prayed to God. He didn't eat a or drink a of water. After this time, He was very, very hungry. The Devil paid him a visit. "If you're really the Son of God," he sneered, "then tell these to become ." said, "It is written: 'Man does not live on alone, but on every word that comes from the mouth of God.'"

city   roof   temple   angel   Jesus

The Devil took him to the holy and had him stand on the of the . "Here we are!" he said. "If you're really the Son of God, then jump off! Isn't it *written* somewhere that the of heaven will swoop down and save you?" The Devil laughed, but ignored him and said, "It is *also* written: 'Do not test the Lord.'"

kingdom   palaces   gold   silver   jewels

The Devil took Jesus to a high mountain and showed him the below. were swathed in and . Treasure houses were filled with . The Devil said slyly, "All of this can be yours now if you bow down and worship ME!" Jesus said, "Away from me, Satan! It is written: 'Worship the Lord your God, and serve him only.'" The Devil quickly fled, and angels flew down to care for Jesus.

Fishers of Men

Jesus was walking beside the 〜〜〜 of Galilee when he

saw **2** fishing boats at the water's edge. Peter and Andrew

had just returned from a night of fishing; they were washing

their 🔳 and mending the ⬜ . Jesus climbed into one

of the boats. "Come, Peter," he said. "Pull away from the shore."

Peter used his ⟋ to push the boat through the water.

| fog | Jesus | nets | night | fish |

A light hung over the lake. "Now, put us out into deep water," said, "and let the down for a catch." Peter stared at him. "Lord, we worked hard all and didn't catch a single . But, I'll do as you say." Peter threw out the nets and sat down in the boat to wait.

A few minutes later, he tugged on the edge of the net, and it felt full. "What's this?" cried, scratching his . "How can this be?" He pulled on the to close the net. He tried to haul it up, but it was too heavy. "James! John!" he called to his friends on the shore. "Help us!" Quickly, the other jumped into their and rowed over.

The men spread their wide and rolled up their

. "PULL!" Peter shouted. All at once they pulled up the

nets and hundreds of spilled out. The men could not

believe their . "Now," asked them, "are you ready to

follow me? If you are, I will make you fishers of *men*." They

returned to land, and Peter, Andrew, James, and John dropped

their nets and left their boats. They went to follow Jesus.

bride	groom	fruit	cake	cookies

Water to Wine

Jesus was invited to a wedding in the town of Cana. His mother, Mary, and the disciples were invited too. It was a joyful time for the and and all of the wedding guests. During the wedding festival, there was a huge feast. Big platters of fish, , and were served. There were also jugs of grape juice and wine.

The people sang and danced to the beat of and the jingle of . Then, during the middle of the feast, the ran out. noticed it first, and she searched for Jesus. "Look," she said, holding a wine upside down. "It's dry. The people have no more wine for their wedding party."

132

six   jars   table   ladle   cup

Jesus saw 6 stone <image-jar> sitting near a <image-table> . "Fill those jars with water," he told the servants. When they were filled, they were so heavy that two men were needed to carry each one. "Now draw out some water, and take it to the master of the banquet," Jesus told them. They dipped a <image-ladle> into the cold water and poured it into a silver <image-cup> .

The servants searched the crowd for the master of the banquet, then presented him with the cup. "For you, sir," they said. When the man put the cup to his the aroma of fine drifted up his . He tasted the water Jesus changed to wine and he groaned with pleasure. He called the aside and put his arm around his . "This is a great feast," he cried, "and this is the best wine I have ever tasted!"

Jesus Calms the Storm!

Jesus was preaching to a group of people when the grew dark and the crowd pressed all around him. "Come on," he said to his 👥 . "Let's cross over to the other side of the 🌊 ." He stepped into the ⛵ , and the men followed him. Jesus was so tired, he went to the bottom of the boat and fell asleep right away on a soft 🛏 .

Then, without any warning, a furious arose on the water. The 🌬️ whipped up the 🌊 until they swept over the boat and nearly flooded it. The disciples clung to the side, their ✋ white, as they were tossed up and down with each swell. The 🌧️ poured down in cold sheets, and they could barely see one another. The disciples shook Jesus until he woke up.

136

Jesus   feet   boat   waves   man

"Lord, save us!" they cried. "We're going to drown! Don't you care?" stood on his feet in the boat. "Why are you so afraid?" he asked them. "Where is your faith?" He put his face into the wind and said, "Quiet! Be still!" The wind died at once, and the waves grew calm beneath the hull. The disciples were amazed. "What kind of a is this?" they asked. "Even the wind and the waves obey him!"

| sun | sky | disciples | homes | dinner |

Five Loaves and Two Fish

Jesus walked through the crowd for hours. He touched those who were sick and wanted to be healed. Near the end of the day, the sank in the , and the light grew dim. "Lord!" said the . "It's very late, and the people are far from their . Send them away so they can eat their ."

lunch   figs   olives   Andrew   crowd

Jesus told them, "We don't need to send them away. You feed them." The disciples whispered to one another. "Does anyone have any left?" one asked. "Not me," said another. "I had some and , but I ate them." ran in front of them. "I've got an idea," said. "Let's talk with the . See if anybody has any food."

139

knees	five	bread	two	fish

The disciples split up and ran in all directions. A short time later, they came back and fell on their , exhausted. "This is impossible!" one cried. "There's got to be five thousand people out there." Andrew found Jesus and held up **5** small loaves of and **2** tiny . "Lord," he said, "this is it. How are we going to feed all these people with *this*?"

140

Jesus took the 🍞 and 🐟 and held them up to heaven. "Thank you, Father," he murmured. He broke them into ∴ and gave them back to Andrew. "Now you can feed the people," he said. The disciples put the pieces into 🧺 and passed them out. Each time they reached inside, their 🙌 found more. When they gathered up the leftovers in the end, they couldn't believe they had twelve baskets still filled with food!

141

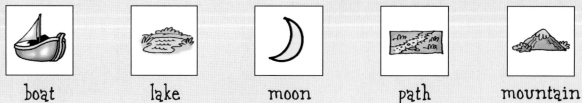

boat   lake   moon   path   mountain

Jesus Walks on the Water

The disciples fed the hungry crowd until very late in the evening. "Go on," Jesus told them. "Get in the 🛶 and cross the 🏞️ . I'll join you in a little while." With the 🌙 to light his 🛤️ , Jesus climbed up a ⛰️ to pray. When he was finished, he went to the 🏞️ , but the 🛶 was already a long way off.

Jesus put his over the water and stepped on it. He glided across the surface of the 🌊 as if it were solid 🧊 and not water. Not once did he sink. When the disciples saw him through the 💨 , they were terrified. "It's a 👻 . Take cover!" they shouted. Right away, Jesus called to them, "Don't be afraid, men! It's just me!"

143

| eyes | Jesus | Peter | boat | lake |

Peter rubbed his , but he still couldn't see clearly. "Lord!" he called. "If it's really you, tell me to come to you on the water." Jesus replied, "Come on, !" He got out of the and stepped on the water. He kept his eyes on Jesus, and he walked easily across the rough surface of the .

wind   cheek   toes   wave   legs

Then Peter felt the on his and felt the water splashing on his . He watched a huge roll slowly toward him. He felt very afraid, and his sank into the water. "Lord, save me!" he shouted. At once Jesus reached out and caught him. "Why didn't you trust me, Peter?" he asked. When they reached the boat, the disciples bowed to Jesus and said, "You are amazing! Truly, you are the Son of God!"

pool   columns   roof   angel   heaven

Jesus at the Pool

One day, Jesus went to the Pool of Bethesda. It was a beautiful of water surrounded by tall and covered with a . People said that every so often an would fly from and stir up the water. The first person to climb into the after the water was stirred was healed right away.

146

pool   eyes   ears   legs   angel

Jesus was careful to step around all of the people by the

 . Some of them were blind and couldn't see with their

 . Some were deaf and couldn't hear with their .

Others were paralyzed and couldn't walk with their . Each

of them waited patiently for the to stir up the water

again. They wanted to be the first one in the pool.

147

As Jesus walked through the throng of people, he nearly stumbled over a man. He was lying on his in a shady . "Don't you want to get well?" Jesus asked him. The man looked at him. "Sir, my will not work, and no one will help me get into the pool after it is stirred," he said sadly. "This or that always gets there ahead of me."

mat | toes | legs | hips | spine

Jesus said to him, "Get up! Pick up your and walk." Instantly, the man felt his tingle. The tingling spread up his , across his , and through his . He knew right away he was healed! He stood up for the first time in thirty-eight years. Then he tucked his mat under his arm and walked all the way home!

mountain   peak   ledge   star   snow

Jesus Shines!

Jesus and three of his disciples—Peter, James, and John— climbed up a very tall . When they got to the , they stood on a and saw the city spread below. They were all alone, and it was very quiet. Suddenly, a brilliant light was shining on Jesus. He began to glow like a , and his clothes were whiter than .

150

Moses and Elijah appeared from and talked with

. When Peter saw them, he was so happy. "Lord," he said,

"it's amazing that we're all here together! Should I set up **3**

?" Just then a bright covered them. A voice from

inside the cloud said, "This is my Son. I love him and I am

pleased with him. Listen to him!"

The were terrified, and they fell with their to the ground. When Jesus saw them, he went to them and gently put his on their . "Get up!" he said. "There's no need to be afraid." When they looked up, they saw no one except Jesus. As they made their way down the , Jesus told them, "Don't breathe a word of this to anyone, until I tell you the time is right." The men agreed.

| house | clothes | money | window | crowd |

The Man in the Tree

Zacchaeus was a very rich man. He had a nice and he wore fancy , but he didn't have many friends. He was a tax collector, and he was known to steal people's . One morning, Zacchaeus looked out his and saw a huge gathered. "What's going on?" he shouted. A man looked at him and shouted back, "Jesus is coming to town! Why do *you* care?"

| legs | shoulders | heads | tree | road |

Zacchaeus *did* care. For months he had heard stories about Jesus, and he really wanted to see him. He went outside and mingled in the crowd. He thought, *This will never work*. His [legs] were so short, he couldn't see above the people's [shoulders] and [heads]. Then Zacchaeus spotted a [tree]. It was very tall, and it stood right along the [road] where Jesus was going to walk.

trunk   branch   leaves   figs   house

He ran to the tree and shimmied up the . Then he hoisted his body up to a fat branch and sat on it. He was shaded by leaves and juicy figs. The crowd began to cheer, and Zacchaeus wiggled out on the branch to see. Suddenly, a voice beneath him said, "Zacchaeus! Come down at once!" He looked down and nearly fell out of the tree. It was Jesus! "Zacchaeus!" Jesus called again. "I want to stay at your house today."

trunk   crowd   money   Jesus   home

Zacchaeus slid down the right away. "Lord," he said, "you're welcome at my home." The grumbled when they saw Jesus talking to the tax collector. "They know I'm a sinner," said Zacchaeus, "but here and now I promise to give to the poor and pay back what I've stolen." knew his heart had changed. "I've come to find and save lost ones just like you, Zacchaeus!" he said. "Show me the way to your ."

156

The Costly Perfume

One evening Jesus had with his friends. Martha cooked a delicious meal, and everyone reclined around a long, wooden . Mary opened a and reached for a jar of costly perfume. She broke it over the of Jesus, then wiped them with her long, flowing . The sweet scent of the perfume filled every room of the house.

157

Judas, one of the disciples, grew angry as he watched

Mary. "Are you crazy?" he shouted. "That 🪔 cost a lot of

🪙 . We could have sold it and given the money to the poor."

Jesus knew that 🧙 didn't really care about the poor. He was

in charge of the disciples, 💰 , but he often dipped his 🖐

into the bag and put the money into his own pocket.

Mary   perfume   money   Jesus   world

"Leave her alone!" Jesus replied. " did a beautiful thing when she poured the over me. Those without will always be among you, but I will not." The disciples looked at one another as spoke. "One day the good news of Christ will be told throughout the ," he said, "and this story will be told also. That's how special it is. That's how special is."

159

The Grand Entry

Jesus left the city and walked to a large, green called the Mount of . "Go to the village down the ," he told his disciples, "and you'll see a young tied there. Untie the and bring the animal back to Me." The disciples walked down the road, and they found the just like Jesus said. They took their cloaks off and covered the donkey's back. Then they led the animal to Jesus.

160

road

gate

cloak

palm branches

trees

Jesus climbed on the donkey's back, and it carried him carefully down the hill to Jerusalem. Even at that distance, he could see the crowd gathering along the and at the city . "Look everyone! The King is coming!" a man cried. "I can see him now!" He took off his and spread it on the road. Other men did the same. Women gathered from the and laid them down.

161

crowd | Jesus | city | donkey | gate

Some of the ran ahead of . They led him into the 🏙 . Many walked behind, shouting, "Blessed is he who comes in the name of the Lord!" 🧑 and the 🫏 passed through the 🚪 , and the entire city was excited! People who didn't know asked, "Who is this man that everyone follows?" The others who did know replied, "Haven't you heard? It's 🧑 , of course, the greatest prophet who ever lived."

162

The Last Supper

It was night, and the city was quiet. Jesus and his
 gathered around a long table to eat one last
together. While they ate, Jesus told them, "I tell you the truth, one
of you will betray me." The disciples were sad and shocked. "Not
I, Lord!" said one. "It won't be me!" said another. Jesus looked at
them. "I'll tell you this," he said. "The one who dipped his
into the with me tonight will betray me!"

163

Judas slowly looked up from the and asked, "Surely not I, Lord?" Jesus gazed directly into his 👀 and said, "Yes, Judas. It is you." The disciples gasped, but they closed their 👄 and did not say a word. Then Jesus took some 🍞, thanked God for it, and broke it into ·°🍞°· . "Eat it now," he told the men. "It is a symbol of my body."

He took a filled with , and he thanked God for it. "Drink!" he said. "This is a symbol of my blood, which will take away your sins." Each man drank from the cup and passed it on. "The next time I drink a cup of ," whispered, "it will be with you—in my Father's kingdom." All of the men joined and began to sing. Their voices passed through the , and the night air carried them into the city.

165

In the Garden

Jesus and his disciples walked down the [road] from Jerusalem to the Mount of Olives. On the [hill] overlooking the [city] , there was a beautiful [garden] , a shady tree, and pathways lined with fragrant [flowers] . Jesus left some of his disciples there, and he continued walking with Peter, James, and John. "My soul is filled with such great sadness," he told them. "Please stay with me. Keep watch while I pray."

166

hands   tears   dirt   feet   bush

Jesus walked a bit farther, and then he fell to the ground.
He stretched out his . "My Father," he prayed, "please take
this burden from me. But if it is not your will, so be it." His
eyes welled with . They spilled down his face and wet
the below. With a heavy sigh, he wiped them away and
rose to his . He returned and found the three disciples
asleep beside a .

"Peter!" he said. The three men jumped up, startled.

"Couldn't you keep watch for just one hour?" left them

again to pray. He leaned over a large 🪨 and dropped his

😊 into his hands. "Father," he said softly, "if I must do this

thing which is before me, then your will be done." He walked

back to find the 👥 rubbing their 👀 . He knew they

had been asleep, again.

168

Peter, James, and John stared at their . They did not know what to say. "Pray!" Jesus told them. "Don't you know that your body is weak, but your spirit is strong?" One last time, left them. One last time, he returned to find the 3 curled up beside the . "Are you *still* sleeping?" he asked. "Rise, men! Let's go! The hour is near. Look! My betrayer is here!"

Jesus Is Arrested

Judas huddled just outside the . He peered through

the and saw Jesus talking to the . "This is the

plan," he whispered to the men around him. "Follow me into the

and watch closely. The man I greet and kiss on the

is the man you need to arrest." The men nodded. They

reached down and gripped their and clubs tightly.

170

Judas branches Jesus smile cheek

When couldn't wait any longer, he pushed the

branches out of the way and signaled for the men to move

forward. "Now!" he yelled. They gathered around him and

marched up to Jesus. "Greetings, Teacher!" Judas said with a

tight smile. Jesus whirled around, and Judas quickly planted a

kiss on his cheek. "Friend," Jesus said to him, "do what you

came for."

171

The men charged forward. They grabbed Jesus by the and arrested him. As Peter watched, he felt the anger rising in his . He drew his and struck one of the men, slicing off his . "Put your sword away," Jesus called to him, "for all who draw the sword will die by the !" He turned his head and looked directly into Peter's .

172

"Don't you think I could call upon my Father to send
12 legions of ?" Jesus asked him. "But the
say it must happen this way." Then turned to the
 of men. "Why do you come to me with swords and
clubs?" he asked. At that moment, every single disciple who
loved and promised to stand by his side fled into the
night. was without a friend as he was led away.

173

courtyard   robe   thorns   staff   feet

Jesus on the Cross

Jesus heard the voices of the angry mob as he was dragged to the . "Crucify him! Crucify him!" they shouted. Soldiers dressed him in a scarlet . A crown of was shoved onto his head. They handed him a , knelt at his and mocked him, saying, "Hail, King of the Jews!" Then they beat him until his skin bruised and tore.

cross   feet   hands   nails   Jesus

When they were done, they made him lie on a huge ✝. His 👣 and 🤲 were hammered to the wood with long ⚒. 🧔 bit his lip to keep from crying out; the pain was so great. He felt the cross hoisted up until his body was hanging upright. On either side, robbers hung from crosses just like his. As darkness dropped over them, 🧔 whispered, "Father, forgive them. They don't know what they're doing."

175

| Jesus | shadows | sponge | lips | drops |

In the final moments, saw the of his mother, Mary, and his disciple John. He heard their whimpers. A was pressed to his , and he drank the of wine vinegar that spilled from it. Then he could bear it no longer. He cried out in agony, "My God, my God, why have you forsaken me?" His breath left his body, and his spirit went to heaven to join his Father.

At that instant, the of the holy temple in Jerusalem was torn from top to bottom. An earthquake shook the and split open. A soldier fell to the ground and cried, "Surely he was the Son of God!" Then Jesus' body was taken from the cross and placed in a tomb that was a A rock was rolled in front, and sat by the entrance day, and night to guard Jesus' body.

177

Jesus Lives Again!

It was just after when Mary, the mother of Jesus, and another woman went to the . They wanted to see Jesus' body one last time. As they walked, they talked to one another. "We have a problem! That is huge. How can we roll it away from the entrance?" They were almost to the cave, when the ground beneath their shook violently, and an flew down from heaven.

light snow guards angel Jesus

He went to the tomb, rolled back the rock, and sat on it. His body glowed with and his clothes were white like . The who stood by the entrance began to shake. They were too afraid to move. "Don't be afraid," the said to the women. "I know you are looking for , but he's not here. He has risen from the dead, just as he said he would!"

179

cave   hearts   road   dirt   feet

The women hurried from the . They were still trembling, but their ♥ were filled with joy! As they ran down the road, Jesus appeared before them. "Greetings!" he said. They fell to the dirt in front of him, and they touched his feet to be sure they were real. His skin was soft and warm, so they knew it was true. They began to worship him.

180

Later, the were gathered together when

appeared to *them*. "Peace be with you!" he said. They jumped up

and knocked over their 🪑 . "It's a 👻 !" one cried.

🧔 showed them the holes in his hands and feet. "Why are

you so afraid?" he asked. "Why do you doubt me?" He picked up

a piece of 🐟 and ate it as they watched. "Well," said

another, "it must be 🧔 . Ghosts don't eat real food."

181

Jesus Rises to Heaven

Jesus and his disciples climbed to the of a tall

for the very last time. He talked to them for a little

while, and then he lifted up his to bless them. While

his arms were stretched toward heaven, his feet left the ground

and he rose into the . Soon, he was covered by a thick,

white , and he disappeared from view.

The stretched their to catch a glimpse of . "Hey!" said one sadly. "He just returned, and now he's leaving again." The men heard a rustle, and they turned to see two . "Men!" they said. "Why are you staring into the sky? The same who was taken from you will return one day in the same way he left." The disciples smiled. They left the mountain that day with peace and hope in their .

disciples	heaven	Jesus	king	prison

An Angel to the Rescue!

The continued to teach about God and the kingdom of , just as had taught them to do. But now the same Jews who wanted Jesus put to death wanted to kill the disciples too. Herod wanted to please the Jews, so he whispered to his advisors, "Find that troublemaker Peter and arrest him! Throw him in , and the Jews will really love me!"

184

Word of Peter's arrest spread quickly throughout the . Believers dropped to their and began to pray. "Dear Lord," one cried, "your faithful servant needs your help. Send your angel to rescue him." That night Peter slept between two soldiers. He was bound tightly with heavy . Fourteen other were stationed around the prison to make sure he didn't escape.

Suddenly, an angel appeared beside the disciple. His heavenly body glowed and lit the dark . "Quick! Get up!" he said and struck Peter on the side. As the sleepy disciple sat up, the fell off his . "Put on your and ," the angel urged. Peter rubbed his eyes and followed the angel out of the prison. "I must be dreaming," he mumbled. "And it's the best dream I ever had!"

186

Quietly, the angel led Peter past two groups of . When they neared the iron that led to the , the gate opened by itself. They walked quickly through. At the end of the the angel disappeared. By now, Peter was fully awake. He knew he wasn't dreaming. "Thank you, Lord, for sending your to rescue me!" he said. He left to tell others the amazing thing God had done for him on that night.

deserts	mountain	seas	boat	guard

The Shipwreck

Paul was one of the greatest apostles of all time. He traveled across many , through many passes, and over many to teach people about God. One day, Paul was arrested for his teachings. He was taken aboard a that was sailing in the direction of Rome. There, Paul hoped to have a fair trial. He was watched very closely by a Roman named Julius.

188

Paul stood on the and watched the toss the off course. He knew it was a bad time of the year to sail, and he had a bad feeling about the voyage. "Men!" he called. "I know that our journey is going to be a disaster. Our lives are if we sail during this season." The guard and the pilot ignore ul. They stopped for a short while in an island , then pu p the and set sail again.

189

Before long, a hurricane wind swept upon them. The ship was driven about and tossed up and down on the wild waves. passed beneath the ship's to keep it from breaking apart. They tossed and overboard to lighten their load. "What shall we ... seen the sun or the stars for days ... kill us for sure!" They gave up all hope of being saved.

190

boat　　　angel　　　bread　　　shore　　　planks

Paul heard their words. "Take courage, men! This

will be lost, but we shall be spared. An of the Lord came

to me and told me so!" Then Paul took some and gave

thanks to God in front of the sailors. A short time later, the ship
in danger .

sur... ...n to pieces by the crashing

waves. All ... d Pa ... to or floated to safety on

the very ...lled ...ot ... broken ship!

Additional copies are available
wherever good books are sold.

If you have enjoyed this book, or if it has had an impact on your life,
we would like to hear from you.

Please contact us at:

FAITHKIDZ BOOKS
Cook Communications Ministries, Dept. 201
4050 Lee Vance View
Colorado Springs, CO 80918

Or visit our Web site: www.cookministries.com